# RELIGIONS OF THE WORLD

# I Am a Rastafarian

❧ JANE STUART ❧

The Rosen Publishing Group's

## PowerKids Press™

New York

Published in 1999 by The Rosen Publishing Group, Inc.
29 East 21st Street, New York, NY 10010

First Edition

Book Design: Erin McKenna and Kim Sonsky

Photo Credits: p. 4 © James Davis/International Stock; p. 7 © 1996 Andromeda Interactive Ltd; p. 8 © Photoworld/FPG International; p. 11 © Ian Steele/International Stock; p. 12 © UPI/Corbis-Bettmann; p. 15 © Ron Chapple/FPG International; p. 16 © Michael Ventura/International Stock; p. 19 © Andre Jenny/ International Stock; p. 20 © Peter Simon/FPG International.

Stuart, Jane.
    I am a Rastafarian / by Jane Stuart.
        p.    cm. — (Religions of the world)
    Includes index.
    Summary: Introduces the basics of Rastafarianism through the eyes of a child living in Brooklyn after his parents emigrated from Jamaica where the religion began in 1930.
    ISBN 0-8239-5260-6
    1. Rastafari movement—Juvenile literature. [1. Rastafari movement.]
    I. Title. II. Series: Religions of the world (Rosen Publishing Group)
BL2532.R37S88 1998
299'.676—dc21
                           98-10416
                           CIP
                           AC

Manufactured in the United States of America

# Contents

# Samuel

My name is Samuel. I live in Brooklyn, New York, with my parents and little brother. My family practices a religion called **Rastafarianism** (rahs-tuh-FAYR-ee-uh-ni-zum). People who practice Rastafarianism are called **Rastafarians** (RAH-stuh-FAYR-ee-unz), or Rastas. My mom and dad moved here from an island called Jamaica. That's where the Rastafarian religion started in 1930.

◀ Rastafarianism is practiced all over the world by people of different ages.

# Jamaica

In 1494, Christopher Columbus sailed from Spain to an island in the Caribbean Sea. That island was later named Jamaica. He saw beautiful mountains, jungles, and rivers, and sent for more people. The Spanish brought slaves from Africa to do their farming. The British arrived later, bringing more slaves. Both the Spanish and the British treated the slaves very badly. Slavery finally became illegal in 1834. Jamaica became **independent** (in-dee-PEN-dent) in 1962. Today, many Jamaicans are the **descendants** (de-SEN-dents) of African slaves.

Jamaica is an island in the Caribbean Sea. ▶
It is warm in this country year-round.

UNITED
STATES

MEXICO

CUBA

JAMAICA

CARIBBEAN SEA

BRAZIL

CUBA

JAMAICA

CARIBBEAN SEA

# Marcus Garvey

In 1887, a boy named Marcus Mosiah Garvey was born in Jamaica. As he grew up, he saw that things were bad for the people on his island. Many were living without water or much food, and they couldn't get jobs. Marcus felt that the blacks of Jamaica needed to work together to make things better. To do this, they first had to learn about their history and **culture** (KUL-cher) as black people. He also thought they had to return to their **native** (NAY-tiv) Africa. Garvey's ideas became some of the beliefs of Rastafarianism.

◀ Today, Marcus Garvey is a hero to many Jamaicans and all Rastas.

# Ethiopia

Rastafarians believe that the first people on Earth came from a country in Africa called Ethiopia. One of the things Garvey believed was that blacks would find a king to lead them in Ethiopia. Before Rastafarianism was a religion, there was **Ethiopianism** (ee-thee-OH-pee-uh-nih-zum). Ethiopianists shared many of the ideas that Rastafarians have now, such as the belief that Ethiopia is the **holiest** (HOH-lee-est) land.

Ethiopia is home to many people. But it is also a place of holiness for Rastas. ▶

# Haile Selassie

In 1930, a young man named Ras Tafari Makonnen was made the new king of Ethiopia. People from all over the world came to watch this great event. But no one paid more attention than the Jamaicans. People in Jamaica remembered Garvey's words and felt that Ras was their king. After he took the throne, he changed his name to **Haile Selassie** (HY-lee seh-LAH-see). April 21, 1966, the day he visited Jamaica, is a Rasta holy day.

◀ The word Rastafarianism comes from Ras Tafari's name.

# The Rastafari Faith

The Rastafari **faith** (FAYTH) grew around the belief that Ras Tafari was the human form of God, which Rastas sometimes call Jah. This is similar to the Christian idea of Jesus as God. Some Rastas also believe in Jesus and read the Bible. Nature is a part of the Rastafari faith too.

There are other beliefs in Rastafarianism. One is that there should be no leaders telling other people what to think or do. Rastas follow this by making decisions together in meetings called Nyabingi.

Having a connection with nature is an important part of the Rastafarian religion. ▶

# Dreadlocks

After a Rasta washes his hair, he will let it dry without combing it. Over time, the hair grows into long, separated pieces called **dreadlocks** (DRED-lox). He will not cut them because the Bible says that no sharp objects should be used to cut a man's hair.

Many Rastas used to live around the mountains and jungles of Jamaica. They wore their hair in dreadlocks. Today, even if a Rasta lives in the city, dreadlocks are a way of staying close to nature.

◄ People who wear dreadlocks carry a part of their religion with them wherever they go.

# What's for Dinner?

Most Rastas do not eat meat or shellfish, like lobster or crab. Instead, we are **vegetarians** (veh-juh-TAYR-ee-unz). Every weekend, except in the winter, my family and I go to my uncle's farm to pick fruits and vegetables. Then my mom uses them in meals. We try to eat food just as it comes from the earth. This is called ital food, or food in its purest form. We usually don't use spices either—not even salt.

Rastas choose fresh foods to eat, such as the fruits and vegetables at this open-air market. ▶

# Reggae

Music is an important part of Rastafarianism. A Jamaican man named Count Ossie used to play his drums at Nyabingi meetings. In the 1960s, a new type of music came from his style of drumming. This music was called **reggae** (REH-gay). The most famous reggae singer was a Jamaican Rastafarian named Bob Marley. Like today's reggae musicians, Marley wrote songs that talked about his troubles and hopes. These musicians have made reggae so popular that many different people listen to it today.

◀ Through his music, Bob Marley has introduced Rasta beliefs to people all over the world.

# Rastafarianism

Rastafarianism came out of the poorest parts of Jamaica, from people who were treated very badly by their country's **government** (GUV-ern-ment). At the time, these people couldn't see much chance for a good life. But today life is better for many Rastafarians who live all over the world. There are black, white, and Asian Rastas. Rastas in different places sometimes practice their faith in different ways. However, we all believe that people should respect each other, no matter where they come from or what religion they practice.

# Glossary

**culture** (KUL-cher)  The art, customs, and beliefs of a group of people.

**descendent** (de-SEN-dent)  A person born of a certain group of people.

**dreadlocks** (DRED-lox)  Long pieces of hair that are formed when hair is not combed.

**Ethiopianism** (ee-thee-OH-pee-uh-nih-zum)  A religion that existed before and shared many of the same beliefs as Rastafarianism.

**faith** (FAYTH)  A belief and trust in God.

**government** (GUV-ern-ment)  The people who run a state or country.

**Haile Selassie** (HY-lee seh-LAH-see)  King of Ethiopia and Rasta's form of God.

**holiest** (HOH-lee-est)  Closest to God.

**independent** (in-dee-PEN-dent)  Being able to do things for oneself.

**native** (NAY-tiv)  Born in a certain place or country.

**Rastafarian** (RAH-stuh-FAYR-ee-un)  A person who believes in Rastafarianism. Also called Rasta.

**Rastafarianism** (rahs–tuh-FAYR-ee-uh-ni-zum)  A religion that started in Jamaica but is now practiced by people all over the world.

**reggae** (REH-gay)  Jamaican music made popular by Rastafarian musician Bob Marley.

**vegetarian** (veh-juh-TAYR-ee-un)  A person who doesn't eat meat.

# Index